This Book
Belongs
To:

_____

Date: _____

Artwork © Samuel J. Butcher

Trust in the LORD with all your heart, and lean not on your own understanding. In all your ways acknowledge Him, and He shall direct your paths.
Proverbs 3:5, 6

And now abide faith, hope, love, these three; but the greatest of these is love.
1 Corinthians 13:13

Oh, give thanks to the LORD! Call upon His name; make known His deeds among the peoples. Sing to Him, sing psalms to Him; talk of all His wondrous works. Glory in His holy name.
Psalm 105:1-3

Keep your heart with all deligence, for out of it spring the issues of life.
Proverbs 4:23

For where your treasure is, there your heart will be also.
Matthew 6:21

*Your hands have made me and fashioned me. Give me understanding,
that I may learn Your commandments.*
Psalm 119:73

Blessed are the pure in heart, for they shall see God.
Matthew 5:8

A desire accomplished is sweet to the soul.
Proverbs 13:19

And all things, whatever you ask in prayer, believing, you will receive.
Matthew 21:22

Let everything that has breath praise the LORD...
Psalm 150:6

*You shall love the LORD your God with all your heart,
with all your soul, with all your strength, and with all your mind,
and your neighbor as yourself.
Luke 10:27*

So teach us to number our days, that we may gain a heart of wisdom.
Psalm 90:12

*Cast your burden on the LORD, and He shall sustain you;
He shall never permit the righteous to be moved.
Psalm 55:22*

But the fruit of the Spirit is love, joy, peace, longsuffering, kindness, goodness, faithfulness, gentleness, self-control. Against such there is no law.
Galatians 5:22, 23

Then they said to Him, "What shall we do, that we may work the works of God?" Jesus answered and said to them, "This is the work of God, that you believe in Him whom He sent."
John 6:28, 29

I sought the LORD, and He heard me, and delivered me from all my fears.
Psalm 34:4

And those who are Christ's have crucified the flesh with its passions and desires. If we live in the Spirit, let us also walk in the Spirit. Let us not become conceited, provoking one another, envying one another.
Galatians 5:24-26

Blessed is every one who fears the LORD, who walks in His ways.
Psalm 128:1

*It is the Spirit who gives life; the flesh profits nothing.
The words that I speak to you are spirit, and they are life.*
John 6:63

*I will extol You, my God, O King; and I will bless Your name forever and ever.
Every day I will bless You, and I will praise Your name forever and ever.*
Psalm 145:1, 2

Be anxious for nothing, but in everything by prayer and supplication, with thanksgiving, let your requests be made known to God.
Philippians 4:6

For the LORD takes pleasure in His people;
He will beautify the humble with salvation.
Psalm 149:4

*Ask, and it will be given to you. Seek, and you will find.
Knock, and it will be opened to you.
Matthew 7:7*

The fear of the LORD is the beginning of knowledge.
Proverbs 1:7

And this is the promise that He has promised us—eternal life.
1 John 2:25

A word fitly spoken is like apples of gold in settings of silver.
Proverbs 25:11

*Now may the Lord direct your hearts into the love of God
and into the patience of Christ.*
2 Thessalonians 3:5

*Blessed be the Lord, Who daily loads us with benefits,
the God of our salvation!
Psalm 68:19*

*And we know that all things work together for good to those who love God,
to those who are called according to His purpose.*
Romans 8:28

With my whole heart I have sought You; Oh, let me not wander from Your commandments! Your word I have hidden in my heart, That I might not sin against You.
Psalm 119:10, 11

Draw near to God and He will draw near to you.
James 4:8

In the multitude of my anxieties within me, Your comforts delight my soul.
Psalm 94:19

Trust in the LORD with all your heart, and lean not on your own understanding. In all your ways acknowledge Him, and He shall direct your paths.
Proverbs 3:5, 6

And now abide faith, hope, love, these three; but the greatest of these is love.
1 Corinthians 13:13

Oh, give thanks to the LORD! Call upon His name; make known His deeds among the peoples. Sing to Him, sing psalms to Him; talk of all His wondrous works. Glory in His holy name.
Psalm 105:1-3

Keep your heart with all deligence, for out of it spring the issues of life.
Proverbs 4:23

For where your treasure is, there your heart will be also.
Matthew 6:21

Your hands have made me and fashioned me. Give me understanding, that I may learn Your commandments.
Psalm 119:73

Blessed are the pure in heart, for they shall see God.
Matthew 5:8

A desire accomplished is sweet to the soul.
Proverbs 13:19

And all things, whatever you ask in prayer, believing, you will receive.
Matthew 21:22

Let everything that has breath praise the LORD...
Psalm 150:6

*You shall love the LORD your God with all your heart,
with all your soul, with all your strength, and with all your mind,
and your neighbor as yourself.
Luke 10:27*

So teach us to number our days, that we may gain a heart of wisdom.
Psalm 90:12

*Cast your burden on the LORD, and He shall sustain you;
He shall never permit the righteous to be moved.
Psalm 55:22*

But the fruit of the Spirit is love, joy, peace, longsuffering, kindness, goodness, faithfulness, gentleness, self-control. Against such there is no law.
Galatians 5:22, 23

Then they said to Him, "What shall we do, that we may work the works of
God?" Jesus answered and said to them, "This is the work of God,
that you believe in Him whom He sent."
John 6:28, 29

I sought the LORD, and He heard me, and delivered me from all my fears.
Psalm 34:4

And those who are Christ's have crucified the flesh with its passions and desires. If we live in the Spirit, let us also walk in the Spirit. Let us not become conceited, provoking one another, envying one another.
Galatians 5:24-26

Blessed is every one who fears the LORD, who walks in His ways.
Psalm 128:1

It is the Spirit who gives life; the flesh profits nothing.
The words that I speak to you are spirit, and they are life.
John 6:63

*I will extol You, my God, O King; and I will bless Your name forever and ever.
Every day I will bless You, and I will praise Your name forever and ever.
Psalm 145:1, 2*

*Be anxious for nothing, but in everything by prayer and supplication,
with thanksgiving, let your requests be made known to God.*
Philippians 4:6

For the LORD takes pleasure in His people;
He will beautify the humble with salvation.
Psalm 149:4

*Ask, and it will be given to you. Seek, and you will find.
Knock, and it will be opened to you.
Matthew 7:7*

The fear of the LORD is the beginning of knowledge.
Proverbs 1:7

And this is the promise that He has promised us—eternal life.
1 John 2:25

A word fitly spoken is like apples of gold in settings of silver.
Proverbs 25:11

*Now may the Lord direct your hearts into the love of God
and into the patience of Christ.*
2 Thessalonians 3:5

*Blessed be the Lord, Who daily loads us with benefits,
the God of our salvation!*
Psalm 68:19

And we know that all things work together for good to those who love God, to those who are called according to His purpose.
Romans 8:28

With my whole heart I have sought You; Oh, let me not wander from Your commandments! Your word I have hidden in my heart, That I might not sin against You.
Psalm 119:10, 11

Draw near to God and He will draw near to you.
James 4:8

In the multitude of my anxieties within me, Your comforts delight my soul.
Psalm 94:19

*Trust in the LORD with all your heart, and lean not on your own
understanding. In all your ways acknowledge Him,
and He shall direct your paths.*
Proverbs 3:5, 6

And now abide faith, hope, love, these three; but the greatest of these is love.
1 Corinthians 13:13

Oh, give thanks to the LORD! Call upon His name; make known His deeds among the peoples. Sing to Him, sing psalms to Him; talk of all His wondrous works. Glory in His holy name.
Psalm 105:1-3

Keep your heart with all deligence, for out of it spring the issues of life.
Proverbs 4:23

For where your treasure is, there your heart will be also.
Matthew 6:21

Your hands have made me and fashioned me. Give me understanding, that I may learn Your commandments.
Psalm 119:73

Blessed are the pure in heart, for they shall see God.
Matthew 5:8

A desire accomplished is sweet to the soul.
Proverbs 13:19

And all things, whatever you ask in prayer, believing, you will receive.
Matthew 21:22

Let everything that has breath praise the LORD…
Psalm 150:6

*You shall love the LORD your God with all your heart,
with all your soul, with all your strength, and with all your mind,
and your neighbor as yourself.
Luke 10:27*

So teach us to number our days, that we may gain a heart of wisdom.
Psalm 90:12

*Cast your burden on the LORD, and He shall sustain you;
He shall never permit the righteous to be moved.
Psalm 55:22*

But the fruit of the Spirit is love, joy, peace, longsuffering, kindness, goodness, faithfulness, gentleness, self-control. Against such there is no law.
Galatians 5:22, 23

Then they said to Him, "What shall we do, that we may work the works of God?" Jesus answered and said to them, "This is the work of God, that you believe in Him whom He sent."
John 6:28, 29

I sought the LORD, and He heard me, and delivered me from all my fears.
Psalm 34:4

And those who are Christ's have crucified the flesh with its passions and desires. If we live in the Spirit, let us also walk in the Spirit. Let us not become conceited, provoking one another, envying one another.
Galatians 5:24-26

Blessed is every one who fears the LORD, who walks in His ways.
Psalm 128:1

*It is the Spirit who gives life; the flesh profits nothing.
The words that I speak to you are spirit, and they are life.*
John 6:63

*I will extol You, my God, O King; and I will bless Your name forever and ever.
Every day I will bless You, and I will praise Your name forever and ever.
Psalm 145:1, 2*

*Be anxious for nothing, but in everything by prayer and supplication,
with thanksgiving, let your requests be made known to God.
Philippians 4:6*

*For the LORD takes pleasure in His people;
He will beautify the humble with salvation.*
Psalm 149:4

*Ask, and it will be given to you. Seek, and you will find.
Knock, and it will be opened to you.*
Matthew 7:7

The fear of the LORD is the beginning of knowledge.
Proverbs 1:7

And this is the promise that He has promised us—eternal life.
1 John 2:25

A word fitly spoken is like apples of gold in settings of silver.
Proverbs 25:11

*Now may the Lord direct your hearts into the love of God
and into the patience of Christ.*
2 Thessalonians 3:5

*Blessed be the Lord, Who daily loads us with benefits,
the God of our salvation!*
Psalm 68:19

And we know that all things work together for good to those who love God, to those who are called according to His purpose.
Romans 8:28

With my whole heart I have sought You; Oh, let me not wander from Your commandments! Your word I have hidden in my heart, That I might not sin against You.
Psalm 119:10, 11

Draw near to God and He will draw near to you.
James 4:8

In the multitude of my anxieties within me, Your comforts delight my soul.
Psalm 94:19

Trust in the LORD with all your heart, and lean not on your own understanding. In all your ways acknowledge Him, and He shall direct your paths.
Proverbs 3:5, 6

And now abide faith, hope, love, these three; but the greatest of these is love.
1 Corinthians 13:13

Oh, give thanks to the LORD! Call upon His name; make known His deeds among the peoples. Sing to Him, sing psalms to Him; talk of all His wondrous works. Glory in His holy name.
Psalm 105:1-3

Keep your heart with all deligence, for out of it spring the issues of life.
Proverbs 4:23

For where your treasure is, there your heart will be also.
Matthew 6:21

*Your hands have made me and fashioned me. Give me understanding,
that I may learn Your commandments.*
Psalm 119:73

Blessed are the pure in heart, for they shall see God.
Matthew 5:8

A desire accomplished is sweet to the soul.
Proverbs 13:19

And all things, whatever you ask in prayer, believing, you will receive.
Matthew 21:22

Let everything that has breath praise the LORD…
Psalm 150:6

*You shall love the LORD your God with all your heart,
with all your soul, with all your strength, and with all your mind,
and your neighbor as yourself.
Luke 10:27*

So teach us to number our days, that we may gain a heart of wisdom.
Psalm 90:12

*Cast your burden on the LORD, and He shall sustain you;
He shall never permit the righteous to be moved.*
Psalm 55:22

But the fruit of the Spirit is love, joy, peace, longsuffering, kindness, goodness, faithfulness, gentleness, self-control. Against such there is no law.
Galatians 5:22, 23

Then they said to Him, "What shall we do, that we may work the works of God?" Jesus answered and said to them, "This is the work of God, that you believe in Him whom He sent."

John 6:28, 29

I sought the LORD, and He heard me, and delivered me from all my fears.
Psalm 34:4

And those who are Christ's have crucified the flesh with its passions and desires. If we live in the Spirit, let us also walk in the Spirit. Let us not become conceited, provoking one another, envying one another.
Galatians 5:24-26

Blessed is every one who fears the LORD, who walks in His ways.
Psalm 128:1

*It is the Spirit who gives life; the flesh profits nothing.
The words that I speak to you are spirit, and they are life.*
John 6:63

*I will extol You, my God, O King; and I will bless Your name forever and ever.
Every day I will bless You, and I will praise Your name forever and ever.*
Psalm 145:1, 2

Be anxious for nothing, but in everything by prayer and supplication, with thanksgiving, let your requests be made known to God.
Philippians 4:6

For the LORD takes pleasure in His people;
He will beautify the humble with salvation.
Psalm 149:4

*Ask, and it will be given to you. Seek, and you will find.
Knock, and it will be opened to you.*
Matthew 7:7

The fear of the LORD is the beginning of knowledge.
Proverbs 1:7

And this is the promise that He has promised us—eternal life.
1 John 2:25

A word fitly spoken is like apples of gold in settings of silver.
Proverbs 25:11

*Now may the Lord direct your hearts into the love of God
and into the patience of Christ.*
2 Thessalonians 3:5

*Blessed be the Lord, Who daily loads us with benefits,
the God of our salvation!*
Psalm 68:19

*And we know that all things work together for good to those who love God,
to those who are called according to His purpose.*
Romans 8:28

*With my whole heart I have sought You; Oh, let me not wander from Your
commandments! Your word I have hidden in my heart,
That I might not sin against You.*
Psalm 119:10, 11

Draw near to God and He will draw near to you.
James 4:8

In the multitude of my anxieties within me, Your comforts delight my soul.
Psalm 94:19

*Trust in the LORD with all your heart, and lean not on your own
understanding. In all your ways acknowledge Him,
and He shall direct your paths.*
Proverbs 3:5, 6

And now abide faith, hope, love, these three; but the greatest of these is love.
1 Corinthians 13:13

Oh, give thanks to the LORD! Call upon His name; make known His deeds among the peoples. Sing to Him, sing psalms to Him; talk of all His wondrous works. Glory in His holy name.
Psalm 105:1-3

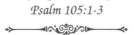

Keep your heart with all deligence, for out of it spring the issues of life.
Proverbs 4:23

For where your treasure is, there your heart will be also.
Matthew 6:21

*Your hands have made me and fashioned me. Give me understanding,
that I may learn Your commandments.
Psalm 119:73*

Blessed are the pure in heart, for they shall see God.
Matthew 5:8

A desire accomplished is sweet to the soul.
Proverbs 13:19

And all things, whatever you ask in prayer, believing, you will receive.
Matthew 21:22

Let everything that has breath praise the LORD...
Psalm 150:6

*You shall love the LORD your God with all your heart,
with all your soul, with all your strength, and with all your mind,
and your neighbor as yourself.
Luke 10:27*

So teach us to number our days, that we may gain a heart of wisdom.
Psalm 90:12

Cast your burden on the LORD, and He shall sustain you;
He shall never permit the righteous to be moved.
Psalm 55:22

But the fruit of the Spirit is love, joy, peace, longsuffering, kindness, goodness,
faithfulness, gentleness, self-control. Against such there is no law.
Galatians 5:22, 23

Then they said to Him, "What shall we do, that we may work the works of God?" Jesus answered and said to them, "This is the work of God, that you believe in Him whom He sent."
John 6:28, 29

I sought the LORD, and He heard me, and delivered me from all my fears.
Psalm 34:4

And those who are Christ's have crucified the flesh with its passions and desires. If we live in the Spirit, let us also walk in the Spirit. Let us not become conceited, provoking one another, envying one another.
Galatians 5:24-26

Blessed is every one who fears the LORD, who walks in His ways.
Psalm 128:1

*It is the Spirit who gives life; the flesh profits nothing.
The words that I speak to you are spirit, and they are life.*
John 6:63

*I will extol You, my God, O King; and I will bless Your name forever and ever.
Every day I will bless You, and I will praise Your name forever and ever.
Psalm 145:1, 2*

*Be anxious for nothing, but in everything by prayer and supplication,
with thanksgiving, let your requests be made known to God.
Philippians 4:6*

*For the LORD takes pleasure in His people;
He will beautify the humble with salvation.
Psalm 149:4*

*Ask, and it will be given to you. Seek, and you will find.
Knock, and it will be opened to you.
Matthew 7:7*

The fear of the LORD is the beginning of knowledge.
Proverbs 1:7

And this is the promise that He has promised us—eternal life.
1 John 2:25

A word fitly spoken is like apples of gold in settings of silver.
Proverbs 25:11

*Now may the Lord direct your hearts into the love of God
and into the patience of Christ.*
2 Thessalonians 3:5

*Blessed be the Lord, Who daily loads us with benefits,
the God of our salvation!*
Psalm 68:19

*And we know that all things work together for good to those who love God,
to those who are called according to His purpose.*
Romans 8:28

*With my whole heart I have sought You; Oh, let me not wander from Your commandments! Your word I have hidden in my heart,
That I might not sin against You.
Psalm 119:10, 11*

Draw near to God and He will draw near to you.
James 4:8

In the multitude of my anxieties within me, Your comforts delight my soul.
Psalm 94:19

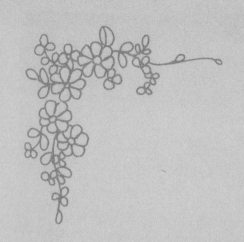